FIREFL

An anthology of writing

FIREFLIES

An anthology of writing

Editor: Charlotte Cosgrove
Illustrations: Carolyn Bolus
Cover Design: Ian Ryan

Dedicated to:

Mia

FIREFLIES

Contents

Introduction – *Charlotte Cosgrove* 8

Fossils – *Debbie Tunstall* 11

The Gift of Birthright – *Sharon Shaw* 12

What we Fear – *Amal Omar* 13

Δεν πιστεύω στον εαυτό μου (I don't believe in myself) – *Panagiotis Soulounis* 15

Letter of Forgiveness – *Shelley O'Connor* 17

Pinky – *Carolyn Bolus (Pinky)* 19

Trying to have faith in myself. – *Lauren Williams* 20

Inking – *David Ellaby* 21

Hopeful mornings, lonely nights – *Yupin Mabbley* 23

Spaghetti Strands, Broken Glass – *Debbie Tunstall* 25

My Trauma – *Panagiotis Soulounis* 26

So far, up to now – *Rhys Stewart* 27

Three Perspectives (A Moment in Time; Confession; The Stare) – *Lauren Williams* 28, 29, 31

Tectonic – *Tom Magness* 32

My Black Hole – *Adam Hopwood* 34

Scars – *Rosalind Allan* 35

Fingers on Lips – *Rachael Silvester* 36

Another Birthday Without You – *Debbie Healey* 39

My Mum Michelle – *Shannon Hampson*   40

A Mother's Love – *Debbie Tunstall*   41

Dad – *Eryn Buchanan*   43

Future – *Kerry Skelhorn*   44

The Marina – *Matthew Ellison*   **45**

A Letter to my Younger Self – *Shelley O'Connor*   47

Obscene – *David Ellaby*   **48**

Frustration – *Tracey Boileau*   49

We all bleed the same colour – *Tia Hagos*   51

Free Thoughts – *David Ellaby*   52

Chef's Specials – *Carolyn Bolus*   53

Turkey Dinos – *Eryn Buchanan*   54

Hurt – *Kerry Skelhorn*   55

Vocabulary – *David Ellaby*   56

Loss – *Paddy Bailey*   57

Looking for Memories – *Shannon Hampson*   58

What I Tell Myself – *Debbie Tunstall*   59

The Cycle Breaker – *Terri Symonds*   60

Eleanor Rigby – *Debbie Healey*   62

Cigarettes – *Tom Magness*   63

Nicotine Dream – *David Ellaby*   64

Stepping on Crunchy Leaves – *Paddy Bailey*   65

The Train Station – *Lauren Williams*   66

We Drink – *Kerry Skelhorn*   68

If Only for a Moment – *Jessica Forsyth*   69

Hope – *Amal Omar*   70

Embrace – *Debbie Healey*   71

Woman to Woman – *Rosalind Allan*   72

Journey to the West – *Jessica Forsyth*   73

Prayer – *Shannon Hampson*   74

Plucking Hair – *Shelley O'Connor*   75

Hands Touching – *Adam Hopwood*   76

All my Fault – *Carolyn Bolus*   77

When the world is in your hands – *Jessica Forsyth*   78

In Morrisons – *Debbie Healey*   79

Words fall like stars from the sky – *Panagiotis Soulounis*   81

Tired – *Shannon Hampson*   82

Mum, maybe? – *Kerry Skelhorn*   83

People – *Kathleen Holland*   84

Life Learning – *Debbie Healey*   85

A Letter to my Child-Self – *Rachael Silvester*   87

Laugh it off – *Debbie Tunstall*   88

Editor's Introduction

This book is a result of writing for wellbeing workshops I started in September 2023. Reading, writing, teaching, and editing are the things I love to do most in the world and the course allowed me to tie everything together. It has done so many positive things for me. The biggest positive, and the thing I'm most proud of, is the people that have come through the doors, the people ready and willing to open themselves up and reveal their truths. Don't get me wrong, there are contributors in this book who weren't as willing, and this is what makes it even more special! Some of the writers you will read over the next few pages had been taught to not speak about how they feel, never to show vulnerability, and, ultimately, remain voiceless. As a working-class writer who speaks with a thick accent and has a penchant for colourful language, I know just how damaging the judgement around this can be. The following writers have talent that I never expected would be there and they have stories that need to be told.

The following pieces of poetry and prose (and everything else in between) will hopefully keep you entertained but most importantly it showcases their strength, resilience, hope and their ability to finally let their defences down. They are the voices that deserve to be heard, they are the voices that never thought they had anything worth saying or listening to. They were wrong. There are writers in this anthology that need to keep writing and performing and sharing their stories. Stories are what connect us, the thing that makes us feel less alone in an ever increasingly lonely world.

There is something in this book for everyone. Subjects that are tough and personal are core to a lot of these works. Subjects such as race, disability, narcissism are all touched upon. In the writing of these works the writers and I have cried and laughed together, meditated our way to a bit of a calmer world and encouraged each other that we all have voices that need to be heard.

The writers here have also greatly reminded me of why I love teaching so much and why it is such an important part of my world. These people will stay in my mind and heart forever and I am truly thankful for those people who have made me a better writer, teacher, and human being this year.

The writing workshops have gone so far in helping people accept themselves a little more than they thought they could. But in this way, it has helped me exponentially. I am more accepting of who I am, I'd be a hypocrite if I didn't try to practice what I preach. I think of the people who I have taught this year in the same way as fireflies (hence the title.) They have been light abundance and shown me the light in darkness more than once. Fireflies are also so easy to ignore in this world, I urge you to now see the beauty in those around you. They've got more to say than you think.

Charlotte Cosgrove

Fossils
Debbie Tunstall

In this world, there are fossils.
They are wounded and wrapped in crystalised water.
They lay like dead hearts; un-beating and waiting to pounce.
Wolves upon wolves of predators lined up in packs to reclaim their power over humanity.

Sometimes, these fossils conjure meetings with others; electing only the natural selection. Although they're hostile and wrapped in ice cold remnants of life, they're determined and omnipotent in their world.
"The end is nigh," bellows the reader.

They know something is about to explode – it's evident to them in that moment.
How could this be?
After all you'd think that these omnipotent things could survive their world ending, right?
Wrong!

You see, these things are nothing more than undignified hearts.
No compassion,
No empathy,
No life.

Their end is near.
Their mission was to bury others – silk stranded aortas beneath the ashes of their supernovas.
They failed.

Because in this world, our world, we are our new beginning.
We are intergalactic fusions that will explode and reform, rejuvenated fossils that are beating.

We are born.

The Gift of Birthright
Sharon Shaw

My goals in life reflect how childhood played out in my life – the child that was once me now seen as a character in a movie. Like I'm sat at home watching my childhood play out on screen. I have separated myself from this child, I am not her anymore. I'm a self-efficient, independent adult with an abundance of love, care, empathy, and support. I have become the adult that I needed as a child. I want to give her the help, belief and support she needed. For all of my siblings and for all of the other children who didn't receive their birthright of the basic human foundations. Instead, they have been stalked through adulthood by a dark entity stripping away even the tiniest bits of hope and self-belief. I am a fully present adult and although my childhood has shaped parts of who I am I closed the gap. I closed the gap between the lack of love, care, and support for my children. I can confidently say that whatever shapes them as adults will never be due to the lack of nurture, support, love, and guidance. I feel it is important to give the gift of love and guidance to children so they can grow confidently and successfully but most importantly so they can pass on this gift to their children and so on. There is nothing to be gained from withholding this gift only tragedy, misfortune, and sad stories you see in the newspapers. A broken generation of children equals a broken society.

What we Fear
Amal Omar

I am not scared of dying but am I scared of not living?
Death is a natural process, every creature in the universe will die. It is reality. Plants, animals, dinosaurs, our ancestors, and prophets – eventually everything must be enveloped by an end.
Death is the truth, the reality, the turning point between our first short life and the second permanent life. My aim in this life is to do as many good things as possible.

But I'm scared of not living to the fullest.
I just want health and hope and love.

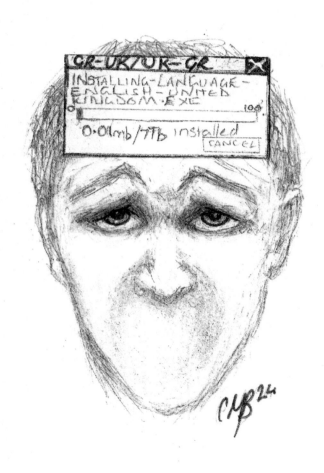

Δεν πιστεύω στον εαυτό μου
(I don't believe in myself)
Panagiotis Soulounis

Will you laugh at the way I speak?
I am afraid you will.
The way kids are afraid of the dark, of being alone,
Of not having an adult with them.
When the English talk to me I want someone too
Like an adult holding my hand
Telling me:
Take your time.

Letter of Forgiveness
Shelley O'Connor

You're my rock, what a cliché, but it's true. I did not understand love, or those throes of passion until you came to me.
Those plans to jet set by the wayside, friends became foes.
I laugh now, we became one of those cliches – you are my one, my soul mate… but the tide turned. The honeymoon period soon ended. Life threw a curveball and the love I had for you waning. Why does life change us? Why can't we be left alone? Let's hide away. Those desert island discs got me thinking. Why can't we run away from those troubles life throws at us? Trials and tribulations that make us stronger.
You were stronger than me, you were the fighter. I forgot to show you love. I took it out on you. Who am I? Who was I then? Who am I now? You embraced me and all of my woes, like granite you wear and tear, but like granite your resilience keeps you here.
We have changed, I promise you, we'll never go there again. Sometimes you worry, things may regress, but I fight for us each day. I promise I'll be your rock, that cliché is here to stay. We live in major or minor key. I choose major to make you stay.

Pinky
Carolyn Bolus (Pinky)

From behind that grey skirt, I would cautiously peer.
You said I was shy, but in truth, it was fear.
Fear from what? Every adult, every stranger!
People were the monsters; you didn't protect me from their danger.
I don't know what to do, I don't know what to say.
I'm not allowed to run; your grip tells me I have to stay.
Panic starts to build, then the tears find their way.
Am I allowed to talk to this stranger anyway?
"What a lovely little boy." Then ask you, the parent, "What's his name?"
Your expression and my answer were always the same.
Your silence prompting me to speak my truth, while you feed upon my pain.
That sadistic smile would always curl, when through angry tears I'd say, "I'm a girl."
"How quiet is her voice?!"
But of course, I had no choice.
I spoke my truth; your lies were louder.
I used my voice; you'd beat me harder.
I ran for help, but you were faster.
I tried to move, but you were stronger.
I'M NOT SHY! I'm fighting wars, abused and silenced, behind closed doors.
My desperate thoughts trapped deep within, while smothered screams drip from my chin.
That night, the skies turned pink, as the Universe whispered, 'Victory is yours'.

Trying to have faith in myself.
Lauren Williams

I am better than I think.
I know I can do this.
I think I'm good.
I believe in myself.
I remember being strong.
I feel empowered.
I want to be happy.
I wish for peace.
I can achieve.

Inking
David Ellaby

The world is in your hands
Lands of flourishing forests
Seas of depths
The beauty like that of a butterfly
Life spans a day
Crammed in everything it can
Fleeting moments
Components of spreading your wings
Wings painted sublime patterns catching the eye
The signature of being alive
Signed by the beholder
The ink of experience
The pen is in your hands
This world is your book so let your pen write free
Never let your hands be shackled by the rest of humanity.

Hopeful mornings, Lonely nights
Yupin Mabbley

Sunset - late afternoon, just a tiny little bit of the golden orange arc. The sun is at its lowest point, but it fails to leave the end of the earth just yet.
Every life in this world is worth living. Everything that moves seems to thrive on the sun.
Don't feel so sad when you see that the sun is going to say goodbye to the earth.
Sometime after the sun goes the moon will rise and show itself.
The moon may not be as strong as the sun, but it will keep things alive.
Some will still complain about the moon not giving enough light for them to continue. I think they forget what the world tries to tell you. The sun is giving light for you to start, and the moon is for you to stop, rest, rejuvenate, to get yourself ready to start again.
This is the letter from the sun to the moon…
It said I think I've had enough for today I have to say goodbye to everything that I shine my light and energy on. The sun tells the moon to look after the earth.
The sun says, "I must go, I must follow my directions, I must do what gravity tells me to. Today is enough. I must go. I will be back. I will rise again."
Dawn comes and hope returns after lonely nights. Everything that the sun touches can feel warmth wrapping its arms around everything.

And this is the way of everything –
light and dark
light and dark.

Blades of grass start to move and shake, chattering to each other. "Get up, get up," nature says. We need to get our nutrients. We all need to live.

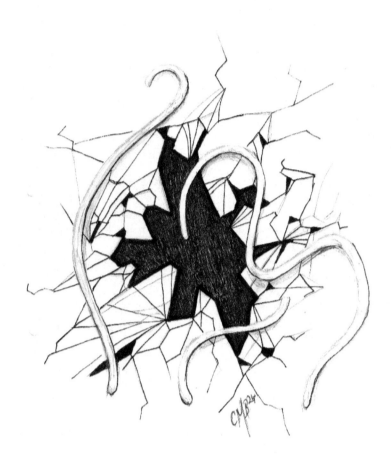

Spaghetti Strands, Broken Glass
Debbie Tunstall

Fibres of my skin.
Blood discharging, yawning
out of follicles – tiny wombs.
And after the scab:
Growth –
Spaghetti strands that spurt
Like broken glass overlapping

It's woven inside me, matted and patched
chequered blanket, all the pieces of me.

My Trauma
Panagiotis Soulounis

Do you believe that your trauma is holding you back? Holding you back from moving forward with life? I do. I believe my shaking in horror is holding me back. Every time I'm in a bad situation I feel like the end of the world has come. When my hands are shaking I feel that everyone is watching me and somehow I believe they criticise me about who I am. How is it holding me back? I don't have confidence like I used to. I used to talk to people without being afraid. It might only be the feeling but I feel it is true how others see me. I try not to pressure myself and put myself in situations. I stay at home so nobody can see my trauma. I buy a coffee and take it home with me because it is easier to hold. I try to avoid working because I fear that, as I'm not a native English speaker, I will be laughed at. Then I'll shake and won't be able to stop shaking and I don't want to draw attention to myself. I'm scared that if I start to shake people won't want to be around me. I'm even scared they'll think I'm drunk.

Even though this is all true (and some days I feel it more than others) I know that I am trying.
For four years I have been introverted with no friends and so my goal is to find myself in the future – to have friends again, be extroverted again and be able to communicate with anyone. I am slowly becoming more confident. I turn up to everything I can so I can learn as much as I possible. I soak up as many new experiences as I can and try every day to be more positive than the last. All anyone can do is try – keep trying no matter what your trauma is.

So far, up to now
Rhys Stewart

I hit rock bottom so hard
I mutated the analogy.

Created a new President, went in
19 turned 20 remanded and spanned it.

Grievous bodily harm inflicted and caused
By my two palms.

Diagnosed with a problem in my
Mind Arena – Schizophrenia.

Seriously caused by trippy scena.

Gotta stay medicated but never
Totally eradicated.

Trip balls anytime if needed,
Two fights inside one
I got beated.
Been there, done that
Got the T-Shirt
Had a fat meal once it was done,
Burp'd it.
Gotta be careful where I put my
Business in, my name is
Rhys Stewart, thank you for
Listening.

Three Perspectives
Lauren Williams

1. A Moment in Time
Lauren Williams

I hand over the gorgeous little bundle in her pastel purple hospital blanket wrapped up like a sweet. A little sweet she was, all snug as a bug with just her little face popping out. Her tiny almond eyes peacefully shut snoozing away with not a care in the world, or the world she is possibly about to unravel. I wait.
Waiting for the penny to drop, waiting for the puzzled heartbreaking face of realisation, waiting for the agonising cry of a mother grieving for the child she thought was going to have. The pain burst through like an alien from her chest. But it's not all doom and gloom, it's not the end of the world. It will be love that will be bursting like a confetti bomb, pride shooting through the roof like a volcano, admiration of the warrior she will become, fighting her way through the name calling and the stares like Joan of Arc.

2. Confession
Lauren Williams

I wish Mia didn't have Down Syndrome. Not for me but for her, so she gets treated like everybody else, she doesn't have to live with people staring, giggling and taking the mick out of her. She doesn't have to fight to just exist in this world, she doesn't have to justify why she should exist in this world. She wouldn't have to struggle with her immune system or schoolwork. She wouldn't get swept under the carpet – medically and educationally. Things would be taken more seriously. She wouldn't have problems with speech or understanding.

3. The Stare
Lauren Williams

It takes a glance
Then a double take
The eyes go wider
I must be a mistake.

You look at my mum, then you look at me
Then the whispers start
Confusion at what age my mum could be
Then the stare

The smirk comes next
The word retard muttered
The giggling starts
My heart just stuttered.

I am not a snowflake
I am hurt
To feel like I shouldn't belong
Then I stare

And pull out my tongue.

Tectonic
Tom Magness

I'm so happy, cos at least I'll see you there, I'm so worn out.
I'm so shattered, but at least I see you care, they bought me out.
I'm so angry, neutral state I'm being vague, they have their doubts.
I'm somebody, she pretends she isn't dead its all the same.
I feel it in my throat, that ball of cancer but I'm a Pisces, refuse to tame.
It's my callsign, a wave of dust, the needs a must, can't find them now.
Just stay honest, I'm on it, I get off they set off the sirens: Calm me down!
Deep breathing... But I... Keep Breathing...
I'm seeping away, you're sleeping ok, you blew up my ego, my lungs will deflate. My colon is flattened, enough on my plate.
It's not your fault as I crumble away...
Tectonic. Dead wrong its:
Here's some roses, another drop of blood cos somebody had to pay.
I'm just posing, smothered in cake, a witch's grave, a working day.
Forced to sweep up, the shallow thoughts, the scars and warts still hug my face.
Fingers thrusting, the frosting ruined, choking clueless losing sound.
Bells stop ringing, frozen in place, cold feet's a shame, and there's the ground.
Nice cathedral, she couldn't wait, the angels play, she finally lays.
But I'm still waking, these restless nights and harboured lights, I sink away.
Deep breathing... But I... Keep Breathing...
I'm seeping away, you're sleeping ok, you blew up my ego, my lungs will deflate. My colon is flattened, enough on my plate.
It's not your fault as I crumble away...
Tectonic. Dead wrong its:
Cold side pillow, I rocked my bed and knocked my head, my stomach churns.
The voices billow, I'm nearly there but it's not fair, the chlorine burns.

More painkillers, can't see the mess that I've become, just stop the hurt.
Sandy beaches, the sound of waves, I know I'm saved, I hope its worth... (it)

My Black Hole
Adam Hopwood

2015 was when my own black hole appeared. Physiologically, psychologically, and metaphorically. As I sat on my couch, my arm suddenly dropped and went numb. I fumbled over my words as I tried to describe to my dad what was happening. And as quickly as it started, it stopped.
This was my black hole.

Physiologically
Doctors discovered a tiny speck in my brain, revealed by CT scan. A small black dot where a stroke had occurred. A malignant event that changed my psyche forever. As well as this they discovered a small hole in my heart which allowed for the stroke. A destructive duo of twin singularities. Two for the price of one I suppose…
A black hole has formed.
The brain forever altered.
But Life continues.

Psychologically
My first day back at college I was a no show. Anxiety had got the better of me and I was falling closer to the black hole. I had teetered closer to the event horizon, the point of no return. Tears ran down my face as I scrambled to form a sentence and catch my breath. I was possessed by fear.
Cracks begin to show.
Falling into the abyss.
Escape is futile.

Metaphorically
A black hole is an infinitely small mass with an immensely powerful gravitational pull that is impossible to escape from, not even light can escape it. As it does with all things though, time kills black holes. At some point in our lives, we all have our own black holes which we struggle to get away from, which seems to drain all light from our lives. This was just mine, which healed with time.
Time is absolute.
Light refills the empty void.
Normality starts.

Scars
Rosalind Allan

Some are like giant chasms in the earth.
Tectonic plates pulled apart then smashed together, never quite fitting again.
Some are dormant volcanos once white-hot heat spilling out
Consuming everything, then nothing –
Silence on the outside but always bubbling under the surface.

Reminders of the past
Scars
We have tried and failed
But at least we have lived
The earth heals and so do we.

Fingers on Lips
Rachael Silvester

She stood outside of the impressive building and took a deep breath.
She couldn't believe she was there.
The large, stone bricks that made up the walls gave the building an otherworldly feel. The intricate, carved arch over the doorway loomed like a giant and the beady eye of the door knocker gazed at her wonderingly.
The three stone steps that led up to the oppressive wooden door were draped with the deceased remnants of the late summer leaves; their mulchy remnants soft beneath her black boots as she climbed.
They chose well with this building, she thought.

She raised her gloved hand up and between her thumb and finger, she gripped the iron knocker and banged it three times in relatively quick succession. After a few moments, she heard the click-clack of the door being unlocked, it swung open with a cinematic groan and a young girl with vivid pink hair smiled, "You must be Toni?"
The girl nodded.
"Welcome! I'm Suzie, come on, follow me inside!" she said.
Toni followed the young girl inside and was immediately hit by the warmth of the room. The aged wooden floorboards moaned as she walked, as though they were trying to warn her: retreat. The next room resembled that of an old stately house. The dark wooden floor was shielded by an oversized, deep red rug and the walls were made up of mahogany panels - which hung various pieces of peculiar art trapped within golden frames. There were two large red Chesterfield sofas placed at either side of the rug, facing each other as though they were bound in a silent duel.
Suzie signalled to Toni, "If you take a seat, a doctor will be with you shortly. Can I get you a drink? Hot chocolate, maybe?"
Toni pulled her black bobble hat from her head and slipped her red coat free from her body, allowing her to see how devoid of colour she was, especially compared to Suzie who looked as though she had emerged from a giant vat of candy floss. Toni on the other hand wore dark grey jeans, thick black boots and an oversized black jumper that had a few white stripes that circled each of her sleeves. She looked like she had stepped free from a silent movie.

"Hot chocolate sounds good."

Suzie left with a cheerful smile, leaving Toni to snoop around the oppressive room. Thick black curtains hung over old windows that overlooked the empty street and in front sat a small circular table with a few letters, patiently waiting to be read. In the far corner of the room stood three glass cases. Intrigued, Toni walked towards them - they were filled with random objects - keys, an old ceramic bowl, a worn leather wallet, but the one that caught her eye was the doll. It had untamed ginger hair crushed under a dark green beret; it wore an itchy brown jumper and a green pleated skirt. A bout of ginger freckles covered its porcelain skin, and its ruby lips stuck out in a painful pout as if this doll had a broken leg.
"Creepy, right?"
Toni turned to see Suzie placing her steaming drink on a small wooden table by one of the sofas, she nodded as she turned back to the doll, she could half see her reflection in the glass and she ran her eyes over the doll,
"it's creepy alright."

Once Suzie had left the room, Toni sat on the sofa and just as she was about to take a sip of her drink, the door swung open and a tall, somewhat handsome man strode across the room. He sat opposite Toni with a clipboard but didn't utter a word - he just scribbled away. Toni sat, unsure whether to speak or to take another sip of her drink.
"Name" he demanded,
"Erm, Toni. Toni with an I" she said as she placed her drink by her feet.
He scribbled some more before setting the clipboard down and marching over to the small table near the window. He snatched up an envelope and what looked like a small dagger, and for the first time, he looked up at her.
His eyes were the most intense blue she had ever seen.
"And what can we do for you, Toni" he said with a somewhat facetious tone.
Toni's dark hair fell over her shoulders as she stared directly into his oceanic eyes,
"I think I have something inside me. And I want it gone."

"Well" he grinned as he ripped open the envelope with the small weapon, "it looks like you've come to the right place."

Another Birthday Without You
Debbie Healey

It's coming around again. Another birthday marking our love and time, our life together. The night before you would always say, I can't believe I have a daughter that's however many years old. I remember when you were born. Decorated cake and candles from the plastic box burnt down to stubs – traces of the last celebration still on the bottom. Numbers and favours marking our celebrations together, marking time passed, marking milestones reached. I remember your face when you put the Christmas trimmings on my last birthday cake, big cheeky grin, so proud of your daughter. Birthdays will come and go but never the same as when we were together. Never the same as when we were marking our love and life together.

My Mum Michelle
Shannon Hampson

They always say never meet your hero. Honestly, I grew up with mine. Watching a woman go through so much and still being so gentle with everyone and everything is a rare phenomenon. It's true – trauma bonds are strong and unbeknown to me that's what would make us so special. I wonder if the fact that she needed to be so resilient throughout her life is the fact that's being stripped away from her now? Her mind is slowly changing, everything about her changes day to day. She's still the same deep down but little by little she's being chipped away at. One of the worst things in the world is watching someone you love lose themselves. I hope time is kind and she has a long ride - surely it will be with a mind as strong as hers used to be. It's going to be a tough fight for dementia to take over her completely. Imagine how much strength she must have to fight so hard to keep what's rightfully hers.

I'll be by your side every step of the way. I'll be your mind when yours is muddled. I'll be your voice when you choke on your words. I'll be the calm as you ride the storm. As back then, that day we bonded, I'll be right in front of you taking out as many obstacles as I can. I'll help you fight for as long as you can.

A Mother's Love
Debbie Tunstall

My mother told me
Not to cry
bottle it up
put the cork in and lie.

My mother told me
it was all my fault
my pain and theirs
a silly comment or a thought

My mother said
never to show hurt
pretend it isn't real
bury it with dirt.

I ask my children what is wrong?
Come here, I'll hold you
For however long.

Dad
Eryn Buchanan

My Dad has a really good sense of humour which I think is one of the best things anyone ever gave me. He always says if you laugh at something it can't hurt you - which is something I took into my later life. I turn people who have hurt me into jesters inside my head and they're there for my sake and no one else's. It takes away their power to hurt me and destroys their control. When my nan died, I spent an hour laughing at the fact that she had just redecorated the living room. To deal with my mum not wanting me I always joked about being a ginger ovarian cyst with enough teeth to pass as a human being that managed to climb out. In total my dad gave me an impenetrable shield.

Future
Kerry Skelhorn

The days are hard and long
We can have all the emotions, even in song
She's angry at the world
Her brain's all in a jumble
I want to help but instead
I crumble

Life isn't fair for a child of her age
For someone who just wants to play
But her brain makes her feel caged
There's no sense of danger
Or even remorse
If she wants it, she'll get it,
Even with force

In time I'll get better
As we all get to grips
Of how her brain works and what makes her tick

The Marina
Matthew Ellison

Entering the fishing village, guided by a narrow cobblestoned, treacherous narrow road, as though time had forgotten, the smell of the sea air tickles the nostrils with a salty kiss. The fresh seafood invites people and welcomes passersby like an old familiar friend.

At the front, the sea stretches out as far as the eye dares to gaze, giving and impression of an infinite blue dessert, full of mystery and adventure. Seagulls make their ungodly cries as they soar above, searching for their next victim to steal a chip or a tray of cockles from. White, limewashed terraced houses stand guard, acting as barriers in case and unfamiliar traveller should lose their bearing and fall from the ancient path.

Below, the marina. A centrepiece of an old fishing industry, left behind by the modern world. Small white and blue boats bob and weave with the ebbing tide, rocking back and forth like a pendulum. On the tough, sturdy, formidable marina wall, there are precariously balanced pots. The pots are made in the old way. Intricately woven strands of rope to form a miniature crypt.

Down by the sea wall, a shop display. Not only advertising the coffee, free wi-fi and ice cream they sell, but also the fatigue of hundreds of years of fighting the coastal weather.

The incoherent sound of the local folk speak in an ancient dialect, no doubt making comments of the tourists as they clamber for safety down the unruly road. All aspects add to the wonderful, magical, and rare life only a few would dream of. This truly is a picture postcard scene that any auntie would proudly display on their fridge.

A Letter to my Younger Self
Shelley O'Connor

Mama Mia! Steadfast, the rollercoaster that is life, what a barrel of laughs. Stop! Stop now! Stop right now! None of that matters. Stop overthinking, overanalysing, just breathe. Why do you care what they think, what they do, who they are, who they rub shoulders with? We all eat and sleep and go the toilet for the same reasons, so why are they any different?
Breathe.
Learn to love yourself, learn to understand yourself, don't chase someone else's dreams. History is in the past. History is what makes us. It's the small things that matter. The natural green spaces, the bird in song, the tulips dancing in the wind. Ignore the noise. Yes, it is deafening but it won't control you, your life, your existence. You'll be dead before you know it. Disintegrated. A shooting star. Pretty to look at (you might think) but gone. Gone in a blink of an eye. Dust.

Obscene
David Ellaby

Lights, camera, action
Nerves falter, stage crumble
Sliced up by eye consumption
Imposing self-imposed projections
Movie critic after watching an advertisement
Got to pow the now experience the wow
Boundlessly bound no more boundaries to be found
The courage to stand on the stage to be seen
Now let's see what's inside the scene's up to you
Just let it out let your reality come true.

Frustration
Tracey Boileau

Constantly bouncing off walls in a room
with no doors, no exit.
Feeling as if my mind will explode,
short wiring from frustration.
Going round and round the room
like the ball that is thrown into the dish when playing roulette.
This is going on in my mind.
It does not switch off,
it does not stop.
It is perpetual, like the universe.

We all bleed the same colour
Tia Hagos

"Where are you from?" they ask, and I never know how to answer that question. I still don't actually – me being born in Eritrea and raised in Ethiopia, and now living in the UK to eventually get my English citizenship, how do I identify myself? Am I Eritrean or Ethiopian? Or am I English now? It's funny how they all start with "E." I guess that's what I am then. All jokes aside, having the privilege of having to identify and introduce myself as all these things, I now understand and firmly believe that none of it really matters.

We are all human, all created by the hands of God. It's just our traits as human beings to classify and label things. I've seen my fair share of what that can do. People thinking they're better than others, different somehow. And allowing themselves to feel and act superior when they're really not. All the unnecessary wars, sacrifices and blood shed that pushes us further and further away from each other. That pushes generation after generation to harm each other based on what they see and hear growing up. All this makes us lose sight of what really matters, the truth. I am a true believer, and I believe no matter what we've done to each other, and no matter how we view ourselves we're all created with the loving and caring hands of God. We're all of the same origin and we all bleed the same colour. It might be a tough pill to swallow for some but that's the truth.

I hope people will wake up and appreciate the beauty in diversity.

Free Thoughts
David Ellaby

Meditation, relaxation, beats inflammation
That be the situation, mind in the present
Open it, bliss of the heavens
Perpetual thought onslaught
Stopped in its tracks
By simple focus on the air bags
The shopping of life
A freebie, thanks Mother Nature
For this free ride
I bow my head
Nodding off to the frequency
Time is no more
Deficient inner core
Explore the pop up adds
Adding it all up infinity
Saturated fat stuck to my toes
Pupils of glass
Nomad cloth stickers sweat shop
Incorporate featured on the trifle
Near a shimmering pond
That cold air breeze, Osiris coughs
Broccoli sprouts fertile fishing ground at home in my house.

Chef's Specials
Carolyn Bolus

Revenge is a dish best served cold.
Yours has gone rancid; it's covered in mould.
A gourmet selection cooked with a narcissistic rage.
Add a bottle of bitterness and a teaspoon of sage.
Poisonous ingredients laced with lies mixed in too.
The toxic flambe delicately prepared with the words that you spew.
With my brain in the blender, you watch with a grin.
Just desserts are perfected so the insanity souffle won't fall in.

Turkey Dinos
Eryn Buchanan

I'm awkward
So much so when I stand I bend too forward
Which causes me to fall into situations that I cause but
Hopefully I find a way out…

Touch wood
Touch it
Be careful not to
Might get a splinter
I should've sorted me gas meter out before it hit icy winter
But I'm a winner
I had turkey dinos for me dinner.

Spaghetti hoops on a loop
Whilst I simultaneously see how low I can stoop
But if you step to me
Just like dinos you'll get cooked
But life's gonna cook us both
And that's just honest truth.

Hurt
Kerry Skelhorn

It's been a bad week.
I went from silence to anger
In the space of a shot.
The words all aggressive
And vindictive
Aimed at hurting each other.
Space was needed but the anger stayed
From voice to text.
Explanations cast blame
There was no escape
Time to calm down
A decision made.
No more anger and resentment
We called it a day.
Normal life resumes
With a hint of awkwardness.

Vocabulary
David Ellaby

Don't be allured by the desolate abyss
Wrapped up as the picturesque
Got to be careful when relieving that stress
Environmental pollution ain't the solution it will only leave a mess
This perilous mucus on my chest
Tantamount to death no less
Need to light up another cigarette to put this anxiety to rest
Flabbergasted by my own thought process
Did I just confess to being a hypocrite?
An insatiable appetite to tell others how it's done
But when it's time to face the music I feel all vulnerable
A plethora of reasons to smash up the turntable
Like a petulant child, unstable mind all erratic and wild
Always falling at the first hurdle causing malignant melancholy
Huge bouts of misanthropy
Combined forming a new amalgamated company called pure depression
Time for some real intricate self-reflection
Diaphanous reincarnate
Into a different mental state
That encapsulates the job at hand
It fascinates how the human mind can extrapolate to understand
It's like an iridescent cloud look from a different angle
See something new turning deep red and blues
Into soothing violets and hues
Now it's time to bust them moves
Punctual with the timing when I'm in the groove
No more death to the music able to listen
Vibing to the rhythm
In unison with the vibration
Beat the addiction into the floor we conquer with defeat
Now we can fly the flag enjoy the victory parade in victorious street.
Complete.

Loss
Paddy Bailey

I've lost something. Something important. Something valuable. Something that makes me feel like me; Myself. This something isn't an object though, nor is it a person. Well, it was a person.

I look into the mirror, and I don't see anything. I am not blind, but I don't see clearly either. It's like a great fog has covered my vision. I have lost something. Or could it be someone? But I said earlier I've not lost a person.

So, what is it?

Looking for Memories
Shannon Hampson

The way my mind has learned to cope is to block everything out – good and bad. A constant state of muddled memories, a protection from the past. I wonder what would happen if I crawled through the pain to find just one moment of pure joy.

...

I'm sat on the couch in my Grandad's house. He comes over so that I can smell his aftershave, but I think he wants a kiss on the cheek. I'm usually the one who doesn't give affection but without hesitation I plant a kiss on his face. The panic I feel when I get it wrong is overwhelming until I see the look on his face because he's been kissed by his favourite granddaughter. That was the moment – one of my favourite moments in this lifetime. My best friend so happy and so full of love.

What I Tell Myself
Debbie Tunstall

Dear unknown,

I want to tell you something.
I need to tell you something.
That girl inside you is a beautiful balance of good and bad, just like life.

She's a perfect paradox of calm and strength, let her out.
Stop hiding in the dark, release her, be free.

Stop hiding in the ashes of your own stones, use those stones to build your towers towards the sunset, and live in the balance of yourself.

Tell yourself you are you and not your BPD.
Tell yourself you're a shining star wrapped in golden garments and be YOUR queen.

Sincerely,
Me.

The Cycle Breaker
Terri Symonds

My life has been one long ever-changing road. One thing that has remained steady throughout, is how I have not only adapted, but eventually thrived with every hurdle that I have had placed in my way. I never came from a good background. I am the daughter of an addict, and a ghost. Looking back at it now, I was every statistic that should have led me to fail at life and yet somehow, just somehow, I beat and, keep beating, them all. Time in care, police involvement, addict mother, absent father, and, pregnant by the age of sixteen. Yet this year I am applying for university, and I am somehow thriving at life.

When I had children, it was expected that history would repeat itself, as my own life was a rewrite of my mother's life, and my children would therefore be a rewrite of my own. But I had other ideas. I set about to earn the title of a cycle breaker and I started a war on the past and on the assumptions that were made on it.

'Just a matter of time' is what I was told at age 16, just weeks before giving birth. That was one hell of a hurdle, but I figured it out. Today she is age 12 with the title of a preteen and has the attitude that would make the devil himself proud of to prove it.

'You did it once, what makes you think you can do it again?' Baby number 2. I was 18. It would seem at this point the plan was still for my life to crash and burn, and no matter how many tricks I did and hoops I jumped though I was never going to quite make it to the next one. The next one always had to be the failure. Today he is age 11 and was sent to me to challenge me. Needs so complex yet I seemed to manage them with ease. A soul like a summer breeze but a temper like a hurricane. Yet my parenting style has been labelled with the patience of a saint.

Today 12 years later I am the cycle breaker. I am one hell of a parent, I am bla… bla… bla... I don't really listen. A compliment from the tip of a knife once placed in my back means about as much as a penny does to a rich man. I do hold a grudge, but they will never know. I worked hard to become the woman I am today, and I offer help and support to the eyes that intensely watched and waited for me to fail. Inside though I am screaming with malicious intent - just let them suffer, but with a smile I recognise I worked hard to be a winner and humble winner is what I choose to be.

Eleanor Rigby
Debbie Healey

This is the smile you paint on every morning,
the camouflage used to hide our real selves from the world.
Eleanor Rigby, the smile in the box by the door.
This is the face we show to the world.
This is the face we want the world to see.
But what's behind the mask we paint on?

Cigarettes
Tom Magness

Spittle in the corners of your smile
Your hand reaches for the ceiling
Dry eyes open
Jaw wired shut.

Skin - floundering
Dead fish in the sea – flaking
Witty jokes are spectres now
Your door is closing.

I loved you
But I hated your cigarettes.
Still 90 years that rigid temper suffered
There's no other soul with a heart so pure and lungs
So black.

I'll always love you
And at last I can breathe easy
Because all I do is take 7 steps back
And drifting on the air you'll see me.

Nicotine Dream
David Ellaby

Fear of the unknown, fear to tremble in bed all alone
Doubting one's own self
Right or wrong can't seem to let it go
Flaring up stuff, is this me calling my own bluff?
Stop pop it goes again like crows in your nose
Sleep sleep. Insomnia creep.
Can the sandman please give me a treat?
Sweet sleep cravin'
Shavin' time off the sheets
Nicotine choking another smoking chimney
In the distant night
Can hear the birds tweeting, soon to be light
Back to the quilt. Slumber slumber.
All I hear is thunder
Thunder and rain two hours sleep on the
Brain maybe next time
Shut eye will keep
A constant battle with beautiful sleep.

Stepping on Crunchy Leaves
Paddy Bailey

Walking down a path, I find a trail. A long trail of orange leaves. By misfortune the floor was wet and damp. Destroying the one thing I love most in the world.

However, I felt like God himself blessed me on this day as the trail of orange leaves leads me towards a pile of more. A big untouched pile of leaves that have been saved from the wet floor.

I did what any sane person would do and ran straight into the pile, hearing the satisfying crunch of the dry orange leaves.

The Train Station
Lauren Williams

This one? No. Missed it.
The children will be alright, they're with their dad. They never want me when he's there anyway. I'm sure he will be just fine; he can survive without me. I finally made it to the station after debating every day to catch the train. For months I would debate if I should go after college.

My chest feels heavy like it's baring the weight of a lead bowling ball, pulling me down into a deep dark abyss along with its toxicity, this time feeling like I'm drowning. Struggling to breathe as if the oxygen is being sucked out of my lungs, trying to scramble a slight thought together like connecting two bare wires to get a spark. Feeling like I'm not here half the time, to the point of having blank spots in my over worked weak head.

It's eerily quiet. The clouds are steady, but the colour of a silver chrome sheet spread thinly across the sky. There is a slight warmth to the so-called winter breeze for this time of year, but I feel numb; not here. The rush of sheer worthlessness pours over me that I can't even catch the train, how pathetic I can't even do that. Sitting down I make myself wait for the next one, time stretching brooding over every little thing that I could at least try to make better in life but coming up empty because everything is a dead end.

The next train comes but it stops, it's not mine. Staring at the sliding doors the past creeps up in my mind like a thief in the night, not wanted but breaks in anyway. Back to easier times, times which I wish I could go back to and start again from there, trying to weave a different life that could have been forged or questioning which path I should have taken. Choices I should or shouldn't have made, perhaps I'd still be here in this frozen plastic bowl waiting for my train.

People start bustling by not a care in the world just trying to get from A to B, wondering what their lives are like and did they take the right path? Are they happy? Or are they on autopilot, not here

and somewhere else far away but their anatomy still sauntering in their catatonic state.
It's starting to feel like I'm waiting forever, people are starting to look at my ruby inflated mug.

Someone gets off the train and I think it's you, suit clad and suitcase. You said you loved me once, but I knew it was as empty as the train at 5am. I stand not quite knowing what I'm doing or maybe it's my own catatonic state. You stop as if you know, sensing. My thoughts come to an abrupt halt for a second then I see the silver bullet I can hear shooting towards me, my train is here. It's my train, the one I'm supposed to be catching but thinking about it, it's the train that's supposed to be catching me.

We Drink
Kerry Skelhorn

The anger it builds
The frustration bubbles
I try hard to keep it contained
But you kept on pushing.

I cannot express
Or communicate well
It's like I'm non-verbal
A complete vocal mess.

I want to explain
Or say how I feel
I'm not placing blame
But it is a big deal.

We drink, you talk, I listen
We drink, I talk, you dismiss it
We drink, we shout, we scream
We drink, we scream, ones leaves.

If Only for a Moment
Jessica Forsyth

Loss can be the end of a story. A chapter of your life that you never get to revisit. A person that you never get to see again, talk to again, be with again. What might be worse than dealing with loss alone is seeing how this loss affects other people. Seeing how it can break the people we love and knowing that there is nothing we can do. But that heartbreak can be overwhelmed by joy, even if only for a moment. When you've had time to grieve, you must find a healthy way to move on, even if it is the hardest thing you've ever had to do.

Hope
Amal Omar

Hope converts the darkness to sunlight
Converts sadness to happiness
And even returns the dead to life again.

At the end of my shift, they call me to the ICU to see an emergency case – a teenager, 17 years old. He came in with a history of a stab wound in his chest. On examination there was a weak pulse and low breath rate, yet he was still alive. Just take him immediately to the operating theatre Dr Nader, the head of O.T said to ring he was going to die. I shouted "No! He needs an operation to maintain his life!" Fortunately, his chest team were available in the theatre. They did operate. It took 7 hours, and he received 13 units of blood. The injury was the root of the aorta, and the doctor did his best to correct the artery. After a few days I saw him walking in the ward.
Hope returning him again to life.

Hope is that ray in the darkness which could convert into a star which illuminates our lives. It is the ladder that we can climb to reach our target, to reach our success. To maintain life there must be hope – there is always life, don't give up.
Just try.
Try and be strong and positive and keep pushing your boat to the best destination.

Embrace
Debbie Healey

Sitting at your favourite place
With tears streaming down my face
You've sent me rainbows
To show you care
I know you're near
And can see me shake with grief.
I miss you both.
The tears are happy memories
Streaming down my face
The sun comes out
I feel it on my skin
You're embracing me one more time.

Woman to Woman
Rosalind Allan

Go to therapy
Blame your mother
Forgive her
Sometimes your best isn't good enough
Forgive yourself
De-centre men
The patriarchy only benefits them
Validation from them is not going to replace what your father couldn't give you
Watch how you speak to yourself
Don't apologise for existing
You are not your body
(Or your body count)
Don't tear down what you wish
You'd built yourself
Call out your internalised misogyny
We were all taught to hate women
You are not hard to love
Self-care isn't selfish
Comparison is a killer.

Journey to the West
Jessica Forsyth

J: Jump at the chance to be freed from your rocky prison.
O: Over the course of 17 years, you will travel. But be aware.
U: Unique is the crown placed upon your head.
R: Reduced from a mighty king to a personal bodyguard.
N: No escaping your new responsibilities.
E: Earning your freedom will take time and trust.
Y: Yet, despite your original disbelief in this trip.
T: The many friends you make along the way will make it count.
O: Once a group of misfits.
T: This is the team the gods trust with your sacred task.
H: However, once you go overboard in your duties.
E: Everyone will cast you aside.
W: With no friends to back you up.
E: Even you, great sage, will be left behind.
S: Sorry may not be enough this time, but not to worry.
T: The team will still need you, whether they like it or not.

Prayer
Shannon Hampson

Why is the question? I hope there is an answer. We must go through things to make us stronger, but why so much? I can't hold on much longer. I'm praying for a break, free from pain for a while, even just for a day where I don't have to pretend to smile. I see so many happy people around, living life so carefree, is that just a front? Are they as unhappy as me? I'm tired of hiding how much this life hurts. I want a world that doesn't suffocate me, a world where we can all live pain free.
Amen.

Plucking Hair
Shelley O'Connor

Pluck, pluck, pluck, pop!
The silky strand of hair
Under the microscope's gaze
Refraction of colours amaze.
The thickness of the DNA
What part, if any, does genetics play?
I think about the fibres and all the different ways.
In plain sight, my journey, my future, my maze.

Hands Touching
Adam Hopwood

Two Gods greet to touch in a fiery amber sky
They await the time where the day will die
Perhaps the touch is meant to show more
Than a mere unremarkable meeting.
One will lay, the other is reassured
The other begins to cry, standing over
Where the other lays
Time marches ever forward
Regardless of what future unfolds
But this is one of a million stories
That remain untold.

All My Fault
Carolyn Bolus

I'm sorry that I'm responsible for all the problems we face now.

For all the wars, the cost of living, and the weather you had today.

It's my fault there's global warming and the ever-struggling economy.

I should've worked longer hours, paid more tax, endured more poverty.

I'm sorry for being disabled, unemployed and elderly.

The NHS is crumbling because of all my illnesses.

I'm sorry the bank took away your overpriced family home.

Because I made you redundant so you couldn't pay back your loan.

When the world is in your hands
Jessica Forsyth

The world is a canvas.
A massive blank canvas
For you to do with as you wish.
Others who came before abused it
And misused it and now…
Now they ignore it.
But you are only young.
What are you going to do?
After school, after college, after uni?
What do you want to do?
Further education? Work? Nothing?
Whatever it is it's entirely up to you.
Whatever you choose I hope
It makes your heart beat fast
Because the world
The world is a canvas.

In Morrisons
Debbie Healey

Pealing the prices off bunches of flowers
Standing in the supermarket
Colourful displays of emotion I don't need to buy.
Baileys on offer, can't tempt me now.
Cards with nice verses
Special dates always remembered.
Train stations with free papers for the crossword.

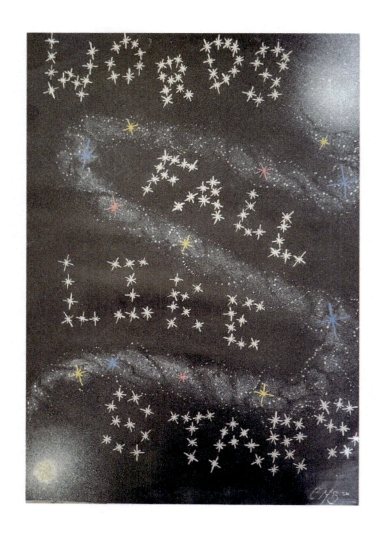

Words fall like stars from the sky
Panagiotis Soulounis

My accent is slow, my words lengthened.
You pull words from your heads
Like fishermen pulling fish from the water.
You cut your words when you want
Like scissors cutting paper.
You speed up and slow down when the mood takes you
Like cars avoiding speed cameras.
All I want is to do this:
I want control of English.
I want words to fall from my head.

Tired
Shannon Hampson

Honestly, I'm always feeling this way. I wonder is it to do with the lack of sleep? Or is it more to do with everything that's going on? It seems as though no matter what I do I always feel like this – I'm placing bets on life tired; I'm placing bets you feel it too.

There is so much going on you have no time to breathe, suffocated by the pressure of existence. We forget this is our first time living this life. It didn't come with a handbook. The intense feeling that we're always failing. There is nothing to fail – we make our own way, own paths, no right, no wrong, yet still trying to escape ourselves.

Let's start to breathe like the trees, calm and strong. Let's dance like flames moved by the wind. Laugh like we're children again and let's love like man's best friend. Cut the pressures and relish in the little time we are given. And then, maybe, just maybe, we will all be a little less 'tired.'

Mum, maybe?
Kerry Skelhorn

I never wanted to be a mum, but when the question got asked, I didn't hesitate. Growing up I was the oldest and became a big sister at 3. I became a mother figure the day my baby brother came home. Age and distance separate us now but he still means the world to me. I had two more siblings who I cared so much about; it was natural to me. So, it surprised my mum when I said I never actually wanted children of my own. I wanted time and independence, the thing I never had as a child. I grew up, moved out, the decision stayed the same. I loved being free and alone but one day it all changed, I met someone - I was no longer alone. Months passed and my phone rang – it wasn't something I'd thought about or planned but a baby needed a home. Would I consider it? It was the easiest yes I have ever made. So now I realise those years of practice have shaped me into the mother I actually longed to be.

People
Kathleen Holland

Sometimes a casual conversation can give a listener the essence of a fellow creature.
Listening to a group discuss whether to give charity money to people begging on the street – some said that the one importuning, probably had another job to go to somewhere else. Probably a well-paid job. And if any of the company got lucky, they might see him some night out on the town wearing a sharp suit. So only a fool gives a 'dropper' to anyone on the streets. Heads nodded and laughter followed but one voice said, "Well, I give. And what happens to the donation afterwards is on another's conscience."
I was impressed.
That person did what he saw to be fit at a given time and in the given circumstances. And there, in the company, in clear, simple terms, he stood his ground. A passing event but the memory remains.

Life Learning
Debbie Healey

I picked the healing pebble; did you send it to me? My journey has been about healing and finding me without you. The journey isn't complete, I don't think I'm even halfway done. What have I learned so far? I have learned acceptance. I have learned about myself – how strong I am. I have learned to ask for help. I have found new friends and reconnected with old ones. I have had amazing adventures – each step I have embraced, some were scary, some were fun. Some I had to do and wasn't sure why, now I'm sure why. I've learned to be and learned to see with new eyes. Don't become old and set in your ways. New adventure back on – I am strong, I am ready, I am excited. One day I will share them with you, until then I'm going to explore the universe and grow stronger. I'm going to learn my place in the world. I'm going to learn who I can be.

A Letter to my Child-Self
Rachael Silvester

One day you will realise that all your 'kooky' traits are going to be what makes you - you.
Stop wasting time constantly looking at them, wanting to be like them –
you will do nothing but pave a long road of happiness for yourself.

I am telling you now to tell them no.
You are perfect just the way you are.

You are different and that's okay.
Embrace it.
Become it.
Let the weirdness swell up inside you and flood through your veins like a river bursting through a dam.

You are quiet.
You are weird.
And for that, never, ever apologise.

The quietness makes you unique, if it unsettles people, let them be unsettled.
What you don't realise is that your quietness is not a weakness, never listen to anyone who tells you otherwise.
They are the weak ones for being unable to sit with their own empty thoughts.

You need to tell more people no.
You need to care less.
Never define yourself by their standards.

You are you.
And you, you are perfect.

Laugh it off
Debbie Tunstall

Isn't it funny how everyone lies?
Parents, magazines, the news.
The biggest liar is you.
Masking your insecurities like a clown.
That persona you carry daily like a trolley full of junk food.

You want to be happy?
Repeat after me.
I'm me.
I'm me.
Thank God, I'm me.

Acknowledgements

Thank you to every one of the writers in this book as well as all the other people who attended the workshops. Without St Helens College and The Liverpool City Region Authority all this couldn't have been done so thank you massively for allowing this. With thanks to Lucem House for allowing us a stage to present these writings in the community. Huge amounts of thanks and gratitude to Ian Ryan for helping to publish and present these works.

Printed in Great Britain
by Amazon